Essential Question
How do we get our food?

Apples
from Farm
to Table

by Paula Kramer

Do you like apples?
Apples are a sweet snack.
They're good for you, too.

Apples have a lot of vitamins.

apple

Look at the seeds inside an apple. You can plant the seeds to grow new apple trees.

seeds

Apples from healthy trees have more seeds.

Some farms grow apple trees in orchards. An orchard is the land where the trees grow.

orchard

Many growers use dwarf, or small, apple trees.

blossoms

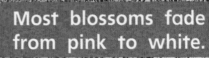
Most blossoms fade from pink to white.

Flowers grow on big apple trees every spring. After the flowers fall off, the apples start to grow.

5

Soon the apples are ready to pick. You can pick your own apples at some farms.

ripe

Many families pick apples in the fall.

bin

Most trees grow enough apples to fill 20 bins.

Workers put the apples in bins. Then the workers put the bins into trucks. But the work is not done.

Other workers must wash and wax the apples. The wax helps keep the apples fresh.

stem

Apple skins can be red, green, or yellow.

Workers place the apples onto trays. Then workers pack the trays into boxes. Trucks take the boxes to stores.

Some warehouses can store apples for up to five months.

tray

People who work in the
stores take the apples inside.

loading dock

Apples usually travel in trucks
that are kept cold.

customers

Most stores have a variety of apples to choose from.

The workers stack the pretty apples. Now we can buy the apples!

Retell

Use your own words to retell *Apples from Farm to Table.*

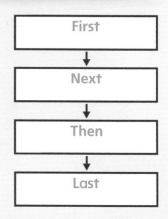

First
Next
Then
Last

Text Evidence

1. Look at page 5. What happens to the flowers on apple trees? Sequence

2. Look at page 9. What happens after workers put the apples in boxes? Sequence

3. How do you know *Apples from Farm to Table* is nonfiction? Genre

Compare Texts

Read about how yogurt is made.

A Dairy Treat

Mmmm . . . yogurt!
Yogurt is a yummy treat.
Yogurt is a good snack.

Look at the chart. It shows
how yogurt is made.

yogurt

Step	What Happens
1	Milk is heated. The heat kills germs.
2	Yogurt starter is added. This makes the milk thick.
3	The milk is heated again.
4	The yogurt is cooled. Then fruit is mixed in.
5	The yogurt is poured into plastic cups. The cups are closed tightly.
6	The cups are packed into boxes.
7	Trucks deliver the yogurt to stores.

Make Connections

Look at both selections. What is the same about how apples and yogurt get to stores? Text to Text

Focus on
Social Studies

Purpose To sort goods and services

What to Do

Step 1 *Goods* are things you buy. Things that workers do are *services*. Look at this list:

apples	pick apples
yogurt	drive a truck
milk	load boxes

Step 2 Draw a chart like this one.

Goods	Services
apples	pick apples

Step 3 With a partner, list the goods and services in the chart.